MORE ALL-AGE TALKS
FOR
*Advent &*
CHRISTMAS

# NICK FAWCETT

**kevin
mayhew**

# kevin mayhew

First published in Great Britain in 2015 by Kevin Mayhew Ltd
Buxhall, Stowmarket, Suffolk IP14 3BW
Tel: +44 (0) 1449 737978  Fax: +44 (0) 1449 737834
E-mail: info@kevinmayhew.com

www.kevinmayhew.com

9 8 7 6 5 4 3 2 1 0

ISBN 978 1 84867 783 8
Catalogue No. 1501479

Cover design by Rob Mortonson
© Images used under licence from Shutterstock Inc.
Illustrations by Steve English
Typeset by Angela Selfe

Printed and bound in Great Britain

# Contents

# About the author

Brought up in Southend-in-Sea, Essex, Nick Fawcett trained for the Baptist ministry at Bristol and Oxford, before serving churches in Lancashire and Cheltenham. He subsequently spent three years as a chaplain with the Christian movement Toc H, before focusing on writing and editing, which he continues with today, despite wrestling with myeloma, a currently incurable cancer of the bone marrow. He lives with his wife, Deborah, and two children – Samuel and Kate – in Wellington, Somerset, worshipping, when able, at the local Anglican church. A keen walker, he delights in the beauty of the Somerset and Devon countryside around his home, his numerous books owing much to the inspiration he unfailingly finds there.

Nick has had over 130 books published by Kevin Mayhew. For further details, please refer to our website: www.kevinmayhew.com

# Introduction

I will never forget the day at Bristol College when I received the orders of service prior to my first preaching engagement and saw leaping out at me two words: Children's Talk. Clearly this was viewed as an integral part of the service, but what exactly was expected of me, still less how I could deliver it, I had no idea. My experience in talking to children was, to say the least, limited, and there was little I had learned up to that point which had prepared me for the task. Had I but known it, no formal training was to be offered in this field anyway, the learning process essentially consisting of being thrown in at the deep end.

I squirm with embarrassment when I look back on some of the early 'children's talks' I delivered, the content simplistic if not down-right patronising. Numerous congregations must have exercised enormous patience as slowly I developed my technique at their expense. Yet, strangely, the person who taught me more about the art of successful communication than anyone else was not a member of any single congregation, nor one of my college tutors, but an elocutionist I saw for a few brief sessions during my time at Bristol College. His advice consisted of three simple tips:

- always begin by asking a question or using an illustration that involves your audience in what you are saying;
- always end with a simple challenge or question that puts in a nut-shell everything you have been trying to say;
- keep the middle short, simple and to the point.

In every address I have given since then I have kept that advice in mind, not following it slavishly but attempting to apply the essential principles whenever possible. They have stood me in good stead. While I have never considered myself a particularly gifted preacher, still less a natural communicator, the talks I have given throughout my ministry seem generally to have been well received. Why? Partly perhaps because my talks were always short, but most of all, I believe, because listeners could always find something to relate to.

Having said that, every talk is different. The style of a sermon is quite unlike that of a lecture – at least it should be! The style of a wedding address is nothing like that of a funeral oration. Similarly, the style of a children's talk – or family talk, as I prefer to call it – is totally different again. When young people are present in church you are immediately talking to a wide age-range, spanning two, three or even four generations. It is essential not to talk down to children, and equally important that adults get something more from the talk than a pleasant sense of indulgence. This is all the more important if my suspicion is correct that many adults actually prefer listening to a family-type talk than a sermon, the latter often being pitched so far over their heads that their thoughts soon wander to such matters as the state of their Sunday lunch or yesterday's football results!

So what makes a successful family talk? There is no one answer to that, but for me the following are all vital ingredients:

- an element of fun
- appropriate visual aids
- 'audience' participation
- all-age relevance
- brief applications
- thorough preparation
- attractive presentation.

Let me deal with each of these in turn.

## Fun

With any audience a little light-heartedness goes a long way towards establishing a rapport. When talking to young people this becomes all the more essential, as there are so many other attractions in our society competing for their time. Too often I have attended services in which the 'talk to the children' is little more than a mini (or not so mini) sermon, and the ineffectiveness of this approach has been eloquently testified to by scarcely suppressed expressions of boredom. Not only do such talks fail to get the message across but, far worse, they effectively drive young people away from our churches.

## Visual Aids

My own preference has always been to include some sort of visual aid in a talk, even if this is simply key words stuck to a board. Indeed, words and words games, as you will see, figure prominently throughout this book. It is a fact that what we see stays in our minds far longer than what we simply hear.

## Audience Participation

Young people (and many older ones too) like to be involved in a 'learning process' rather than simply being talked to. Games, word-searches, quizzes and other such forms of participation offer an effective way of including the congregation in what you are saying. We need to promote an atmosphere in which people feel part of what is going on.

## All-age Relevance

As I have said already, many adults are actually far more receptive to a talk geared towards a younger audience than they are to a sermon. Many also enjoy participation as much as children, if not more so! Even if this were not the case, we owe it to any congregation to ensure that a talk is able both to stimulate and challenge.

## Brief Applications

I have always believed that the secret of a successful family talk is to keep the application – the serious bit at the end – as short and simple as possible. Ideally, the message you are looking to put across (and this ought to be one message, not several) should speak for itself through the illustrations and visual aids you use, though some expansion of what this means is usually necessary. Overdo the application and you will pay the price. Which of us hasn't witnessed the sudden glazed looks the moment the 'religious' part of a talk is reached. Whatever you do, don't try and ram the point home; if you haven't made the point through the fun part of your talk, you won't make it afterwards.

## Thorough Preparation

There is no getting away from it: talking to young people takes time. There were many occasions during my ministry when I spent longer preparing a single family talk (even one lasting a mere five minutes) than two full-length sermons. In this book I have attempted to do most of the spadework for you through suggesting ideas and ways of presenting these, but to deliver most of the talks you will still need to spend some time in preparation. Don't be put off by this. The effort may occasionally seem out of proportion to the time taken up by the talk during the service, but I believe the results will more than justify it. What you put in, you will get out.

## Attractive Presentation

In this sophisticated age, young people as much as adults are used to slick, glossy and professional presentations. While we cannot emulate these, it is important for visual material to be as clear and well presented as possible. Home computers and modern technology make this far easier to achieve than it once was, as well as saving huge amounts of time. While material can be written out by hand (for many of these talks I did just that), I would strongly recommend the use of a PC word-processing package if possible. When it comes to displaying material, my own preference, arrived at after several years of trial and error, was to use a magnetic whiteboard in conjunction with magnetic tape (available through most office stationery suppliers), with the back-up of a second whiteboard (magnetic or otherwise) and sticky tack. If you choose this method, you will need easels for these, as light and portable as possible. A supply of thick coloured marker pens (in washable and permanent ink) is a must for many talks, as is a copious supply of thin card and/or paper. Many of the talks nowadays could be delivered using an overhead projector and screen if this is preferred to board and easel. Adapt to your available resources. On a purely practical note, make use of a radio microphone if this is available. Family talks often involve a degree of movement, and it is all too easy to stray from a standing microphone so that you become inaudible, or, worse still, to trip headlong over the wires of a halterneck model! (The younger members of the congregation will delight in this, but for you it can prove embarrassing and even dangerous.) Each talk in this collection is set out according to a basic framework:

- a suggested Bible passage which should normally be read publicly prior to the talk
- a statement of the aim of the talk
- details of preparation needed beforehand
- the talk itself.

This last section includes instructions relating, for example, to the use of illustrations, together with a suggested application of the talk. The talks will work best if, having read and digested these paragraphs, you present them in your own words. This is particularly true where the congregation is invited to respond, and developing and incorporating their ideas and answers into the talk will require a measure of ad-libbing on your part.

Each of the talks in this booklet was used in public worship during my time in the ministry. No doubt many are flawed in places and could be considerably improved – I do not offer them as examples of how it should be done, but rather as a resource which may be of help to you. Of all the comments received during my ministry, few have gratified me more than those when young people have referred in conversation to talks I delivered three, four, even five years back. Whether they remembered the point I had been making I cannot say, but, whatever else, they clearly enjoyed being in church and carried away positive associations of their time there. That in itself was always sufficient motivation to spend further time and energy devoted to getting the message across.

*Nick Fawcett*

# Advent

# Prepared for His Coming

**Readings**   Isaiah 40:1-11; Luke 1:57-79

**Aim**   To emphasise that the message of Advent is as much about the present – the way we live, think and feel now – as about the future.

**Preparation**   You will need the following as visual aids: potato peeler, sun cream, recipe book, holiday brochure, GCSE revision book, sandpaper, soap and bowl of water, can of oil, Moses basket, safety glasses/goggles, umbrella, shin pads, cricket gloves or pads.

**Talk**   Display the items you assembled beforehand, and ask if anyone can identify what they have in common. It is most unlikely that anybody will have a clue. Announce that you have some questions that will help provide the missing link.

1. Which of the items might you use if you were planning to spend a day on the beach in the middle of summer? *(Sun cream)*

2. Which might you take if it was going to rain? *(Umbrella)*

3. Which might you use if you were going to work with machinery? *(Safety glasses/goggles)*

4. Which might you buy if you or your partner were expecting a baby? *(Moses basket)*

5. What should you check in your car engine before going on a long journey? *(Oil)*

6. Which should you use before sitting down for a meal? *(Soap and water)*

7. Which do you need to use before you start painting a peeling door or windowsill? *(Sandpaper)*

8. Which would you need to study before sitting an exam? *(GCSE revision book)*

9. Which might you look at if you're planning to go away on holiday? *(Holiday brochure)*

10. Which might you need to look at if you're planning a special meal? *(Recipe book)*

11. Which might you use if you're planning to have chips for lunch? *(Potato peeler)*

12. Which would you use to plant some potatoes? *(Spade)*

13. What might you put on before playing a serious game of football? *(Shin pads)*

14. What might you wear if you're playing a game of cricket? *(Cricket gloves/pads)*

Once all the questions have been answered, ask if anyone has guessed what all the items have in common. If people are still unsure, suggest the motto of the Boy Scouts as a clue – 'Be prepared'. All of the items remind us how important it is to prepare for something in advance. We wouldn't go away on holiday without deciding first where to stay. We wouldn't have much chance of passing an exam if we didn't revise first. We wouldn't make a very good job of decorating if we didn't sand down the area before painting it. We'd risk serious injury playing cricket or football without shin pads or cricket gloves, and similarly if we used machinery without safety glasses. We'd suffer serious sunburn if we lay on a beach without sun cream, and we'd experience a real soaking in a thunderstorm without an umbrella. So often, for a host of reasons, it's vital to prepare for the future, to plan ahead, and that is precisely the message in both our readings today.

First, words spoken three thousand years ago by the prophet Isaiah: 'A voice cries out: "In the wilderness prepare the way of the Lord, make straight in the desert a highway for our God"' (Isaiah 40:3). Isaiah tells the people of Israel to be ready for the coming of the Messiah, the one God is sending to deliver his people, and, almost a thousand years later, those words were to take on new meaning following the birth of a child called John, later to be known as John the Baptist.

And you, child, will be called the prophet of the Most High; for you will go before the Lord to prepare his ways, to give knowledge of salvation to his people by the forgiveness of their sins. (Luke 1:76)

Words spoken by John's father, Zechariah, through which he gave thanks to God that his son was to prepare the way of Jesus. Which, of course, is just what he did, preaching and teaching in the wilderness so that people would be ready to welcome the Messiah when he came. Here is one of the great truths at the heart of Advent – the fact that God prepared the way for his coming in Christ. Through the words of the prophets centuries back in history, and through so much else in scripture, he revealed his loving purpose so that the world might be ready to welcome him. Yet, as the Apostle John reminds us, many failed to do so, either misreading the signs or preferring their own way to the way of Christ. The coming of Jesus caught them unprepared.

Advent asks us whether we have responded and whether we are any more ready today. Have we listened to God's promises? Have we understood what they mean? Have we opened our lives to his love in Christ? Above all, do we live in such a way that we would be happy to welcome him should he return here and now, or at any moment? No doubt we are all busy preparing for Christmas, buying presents, writing cards, decorating the Christmas tree, planning meals and get-togethers. All of these have their place as part of our celebrations, but Advent asks us, how ready are we to celebrate what this time of year is all about: the birth of Jesus Christ and the new life his coming offers to all?

# Recognising the Signs

**Reading**  Matthew 11:2-27

**Aim**  To remind us that there are signs of the coming of God's kingdom, if only we have the faith to believe and a willingness to see.

**Preparation**  First, reproduce each of the following map symbols on a large sheet of card / paper (one per sheet). Larger versions of these pictures, suitable for enlarging and photocopying, may be found on pages 19-20.

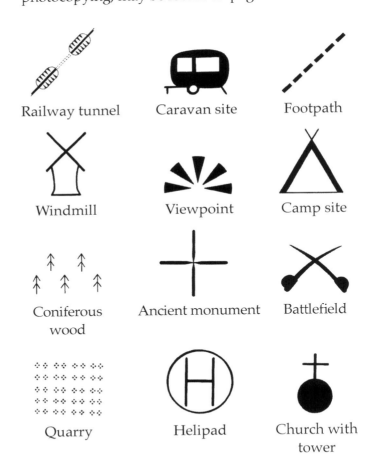

| | | |
|---|---|---|
| Railway tunnel | Caravan site | Footpath |
| Windmill | Viewpoint | Camp site |
| Coniferous wood | Ancient monument | Battlefield |
| Quarry | Helipad | Church with tower |

Have each of the pictures ready to display during the talk.

**Talk** Hold up a copy of an Ordnance Survey map and tell the congregation that you want to test their knowledge of the symbols used on maps. One by one, display the pictures you have prepared, asking if anyone can identify what the symbols mean.

Each of these, of course, is only a sign, but all of them point to a reality, and when we have only a map to guide us, then these symbols become vitally important. Interpret them correctly and we will find the way we are looking for; misunderstand them and we will end up hopelessly lost.

John the Baptist began to wonder if he'd misunderstood things, as he lay in prison following his arrest by Herod. He had believed Jesus was the one sent by God to establish his promised kingdom, but now he wasn't so sure, wondering if perhaps he'd misread the signs, so he sent some of his own disciples to question Jesus. The reply they gave set his mind at rest:

> Jesus answered them, 'Go and tell John what you hear and see: the blind receive their sight, the lame walk, the lepers are cleansed, the deaf hear, the dead are raised, and the poor have good news brought to them.' (Matthew 11:4-5)

It was all that John needed to know, for here were signs pointing unmistakably to the dawn of God's kingdom.

If Jesus' coming was the dawn, however, the fulfilment of that kingdom is yet to come. Advent reminds us that this fulfilment will take place; that Jesus will return to finish what he started and to complete God's purpose. It is easy to get hung up on signs of his coming, on the various portents that may indicate the day is near. Many have done just that, claiming that the last times are upon us, only to be proved wrong. Advent, by contrast, does not call us to focus on the future but instead to live in the present assured that the future is in God's hands. It calls us to look at what God is doing among us, to glimpse the work of Jesus here and now through his Spirit, and to share in that work through our love and witness.

The signs are here all around us, if only we are ready to see. Look at what God has done for you. Look at what he has done for others. Look at what he has done and is doing through Christ, and so trust that his will shall be done and his kingdom come.

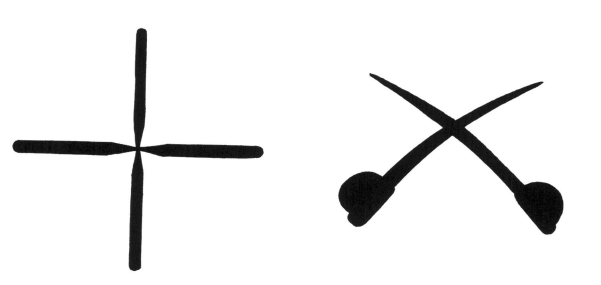

19

# Knowing the Bible

**Readings**  Psalm 119:105-112; John 1:14-18

**Aim**  To bring home that the Bible is not simply a book about the past, but applies to every one of us, every day.

**Preparation**  Display on a whiteboard or OHP the following riddle so that it can be seen by the entire congregation:

> My first is in BETHLEHEM
> but not in the INN.
> My second's in ISRAEL
> and also in KING.
> My third is in BABY –
> a gift from ABOVE.
> My fourth is in RULER
> and seen in his LOVE.
> My last is in EVERYTHING
> though not seen in FULL.
> The word I am seeking
> applies to us all.

**Talk**  Tell the congregation that you are going to give various instructions, which you want them to listen to carefully and then to respond as appropriate.

- Anyone with blue eyes, shout 'Me!'
- Anyone born in April, stand up
- Anyone who walked to church, cough loudly
- Anyone 10 or under, wave your left hand
- Anyone aged 11 or over, wave your right hand
- Anyone who's watched *The Lord of the Rings* (you may prefer to substitute a more recently released film), nod your head
- Anyone with two heads, nod them both at once!
- Anyone under five foot tall, wiggle your legs

- Anyone with good hearing, wiggle your ears!
- Anyone with black hair, pat your head
- Anyone who doesn't like cabbage, shake your head
- Anyone whose favourite colour is red, lift both hands in the air
- Anyone born in this town, cheer
- Anyone who's strong, flex your muscles
- Anyone who's feeling hungry, lick your lips
- Anyone who can touch their toes, wink an eye
- Anyone who thinks this quiz is going on for too long, yawn!

Ask how many people responded every time? The answer, of course, is no one. Some of the instructions applied to just a few of us, some to none at all, and some to many, but there was nobody to whom all of them applied. That's not surprising, of course, because we're all different, no two people exactly the same, not even if they're twins. Take a look, though, at our Advent riddle (display the riddle you prepared beforehand). Can anyone work out the answer? (It is, of course, BIBLE; offer help in solving this, if needed.) Who is the riddle actually about? *(Jesus.)* So why is the riddle about one thing but its answer another? The answer lies in words from our second reading:

> 'And the Word became flesh and lived among us, and we have seen his glory, the glory as of a father's only son, full of grace and truth' (John 1:14-15a).

According to John, what we have here (hold up Bible) is embodied in Jesus. In other words, everything in the Bible is concerned ultimately with him, pointing in some way to his coming, his nature, his calling or his kingdom.

Advent, then, is a time that reminds us of the importance of reading God's word – not just the story of Jesus' birth or simply the Gospels, but all scripture, for through it God speaks not just of the past but of the present and the future; not just to people long ago but to us today. It calls us equally to respond to Jesus, the Word made flesh, the one who came in fulfilment of prophecy and God's promises to bring forgiveness and new life to all. Those too apply as much to you and me today as to those he first came to. Whoever we are, the message of God's coming in Christ applies to us all!

# Meeting Jesus

**Reading**   John 20:30-31

**Aim**   To emphasise that in the Bible, the word of God, we encounter Jesus, the Word made flesh.

**Preparation**   No advance preparation is needed for this talk.

**Talk**
- In which book do we meet Man Friday? *(Robinson Crusoe)*
- In which series of books do we meet Piglet, Christopher Robin and Eeyore? *(Winnie the Pooh)*
- In which books do we meet Mr Angry, Mr Happy and Mr Lazy? *(Mr Men)*
- What book tells of the Queen of Hearts, White Rabbit and Mad Hatter? *(Alice's Adventures in Wonderland)*
- In which book do we meet Mowgli, Baloo, and Shere Khan? *(The Jungle Book)*
- In which comic do we meet Dennis the Menace, Minnie the Minx and Roger the Dodger? *(The Beano)*
- In which books do we meet Dick, Julian, Anne, George and Timmy? *(The Enid Blyton 'Famous Five' books)*
- In which books do we encounter Bramwell Brown, Jolly Tall and Ruff? *(The 'Old Bear' books)*
- In which book do we meet Fagin and the Artful Dodger? *(Oliver Twist)*
- In which book do we meet Ratty, Mr Badger and Toad of Toad Hall? *(The Wind in the Willows)*
- In which books do we meet Martha Monkey, Dinah Doll, Mr Plod and Sly the goblin? *(Noddy)*
- In which book do we meet Catherine Earnshaw and Heathcliff? *(Wuthering Heights)*

These are all books in which we meet particular characters, though of course none of them are real, each having been invented by the author. To 'meet' a real person, we need to read an autobiography, a book in which somebody tells the story of his or her life or experiences. Who can identify the authors of the following (you may prefer to substitute your own titles)?

- *Moonwalk* (Michael Jackson)
- *Autobiographical Notes* (Albert Einstein)
- *A Long Walk to Freedom* (Nelson Mandela)
- *Dreams from My Father* (Barack Obama)
- *Confessions of an Heiress* (Paris Hilton)
- *The Downing Street Years* (Margaret Thatcher)
- *The Diary of a Young Girl* (Anne Frank)

In these books we encounter and learn something about real people to the point that we feel we know something about them, but, of course, we don't actually know them any more than they know us. One book, though, is different, and that's the Bible. In this book there is someone we do not simply come to know about, but one whom we can know personally: Jesus, the Word made flesh. As the Apostle John puts it at end of his Gospel:

> Jesus did many other signs in the presence of his disciples, which are not written in this book. But these are written so that you may come to believe that Jesus is the Messiah, the Son of God, and that through believing you may have life in his name. (John 20:30-31)

# RSVP

**Reading**    Mark 1:1-8

**Aim**    To stress that the most important thing about Christmas is our response, and to show how Mark, through starting his Gospel with the ministry of John the Baptist rather than the Christmas story, brings home this point.

**Preparation**    Using large letters on a whiteboard or OHP display the following abbreviations:

PTO, SWALK, TTFN, ASAP, OHMS, NIMBY, AWOL, WYSIWYG, AKA, HAND, ATB, BRB, LOL, RSVP

Next – using your own drawings, enlarged cut-outs from old Christmas cards or material from a Christmas clip-art package – prepare the following pictures on large sheets of paper. Display these, together with four blank sheets of paper, around the church.

*Angels*
*Three kings/wise men*
*Blank sheet of paper*
*Baby*
*Shepherds*
*Single angel (Gabriel)*
*Blank sheet of paper*
*Manger*
*Blank sheet of paper*
*Bethlehem (idealised silhouette)*
*Mary (Madonna and child)*
*Blank sheet of paper*
*Joseph*

Finally, depending on which method you want to use, prime your church organist to play the first lines of the following carols during the talk, or secure a recording of each on tape or CD, ensuring that you are able to skip easily to the first line of each as required. (If you enlist the help of your organist, you will need to plan carefully to ensure that the right piece is played, or silence observed, at the right time during the talk.)

Angels from the realms of glory

We three kings of Orient are

**Five seconds of silence!**

Unto us a son is born

While shepherds watched

The angel Gabriel from heaven came

**Five seconds of silence!**

Away in a manger

**Five seconds of silence!**

Once in royal David's city

The Virgin Mary had a baby boy

**Five seconds of silence!**

Joseph was an old man

**Talk**  Tell the congregation that you want to start by testing their knowledge of abbreviations. Display the list you prepared earlier, and ask if anyone can identify what each initial stands for.

PTO *(Please turn over)*

SWALK *(Sealed with a loving kiss)*

TTFN *(Ta ta for now)*

ASAP *(As soon as possible)*

OHMS *(On Her Majesty's Service)*

NIMBY *(Not in my backyard)*

AWOL *(Absent without leave)*

WYSIWYG *(What you see is what you get)*

AKA *(Also known as)*

HAND *(Have a nice day)*

ATB *(All the best)*

BRB *(Be right back)*

LOL *(Loads of laughs or laughing out loud)*

RSVP *(Répondez s'il vous plait or please respond)*

What has all this to do with Mark's Gospel? The answer is that each of these says something different, and so does the way that Mark starts his Gospel. Tell the congregation that it's the last of these abbreviations that particularly concerns you, and that you have a second quiz, this time a musical one, that will help explain why. The aim of the quiz is to compare the way Matthew, Mark and Luke open their accounts of the life and ministry of Jesus. (Point out that you have not included John's Gospel because it is unlike the other Gospels, recording several events that they do not mention and approaching things in a slightly different way.) Explain that you (or the organist) will play a musical clue, after which you will call out the name of one of the Gospel writers (see the list on the next page). The aim of the quiz is then to match the tune and Gospel to one of the pictures displayed around the church.

| GOSPEL | CLUE | PICTURE |
|---|---|---|
| Luke | Angels from the realms of glory | Angels |
| Matthew | We three kings of Orient are | Three kings/ wise men |
| Mark | **Five seconds of silence!** | Blank sheet of paper |
| Matthew | Unto us a son is born | Baby |
| Luke | While shepherds watched | Shepherds |
| Luke | The angel Gabriel from | Single angel (Gabriel) |
| Mark | **Five seconds of silence!** | Blank sheet of paper |
| Luke | Away in a manger | Manger |
| Mark | **Five seconds of silence!** | Blank sheet of paper |

| | | |
|---|---|---|
| Luke | Once in royal David's city | Bethlehem (silhouette) |
| Luke | The virgin Mary had a baby boy | Mary (Madonna and child) |
| Mark | **Five seconds of silence!** | Blank sheet of paper |
| Matthew | Joseph was an old man | Joseph |

Luke, then, tells us about the angel visiting Mary, the birth in a stable and laying of Jesus in a manger, shepherds in the fields and a multitude of angels praising God. Matthew tells us about the angel visiting Joseph, about a child born who will be called God with us, and about wise men bringing their gifts. How about Mark – what does he tell us? The answer, of course, is nothing, yet in another sense he tells us everything, for he starts his Gospel not in Bethlehem or Nazareth but with the preaching of John the Baptist, calling people to turn away from their old life in readiness to welcome the promised Messiah. In doing so he reminds us straightaway of perhaps the most important message of Christmas – that the coming of Jesus into the world calls for a response. In Matthew, the response is from Joseph and the wise men, Joseph accepting Mary as his wife and the wise men journeying from the East to present their gifts. In Luke, the response is from Mary, accepting that with God nothing is impossible. Mark, though, turns the spotlight firmly on the reader – on you and me – asking, through John the Baptist, the simple but vital question: how do you respond to God's coming among us? RSVP!

# As White as Snow

**Readings**    Psalm 51:1-12; Isaiah 1:12-20; Matthew 1:18-25

**Aim**    To highlight the transformation that Jesus is able to bring about in our lives.

**Preparation**    Cut out a picture from a calendar depicting a winter's snow scene. Stick this on to a whiteboard or wall in the church, and cover with a large sheet of blank white paper. Next, copy and enlarge the following shapes (larger versions may be found on page 32, or draw your own freehand):

Practise putting these together to form a snowman, as follows:

Fix a piece of sticky tack to the back of each piece and retain for use during the talk.

**Talk** Tell the congregation that you have prepared a picture for them. Point to the blank paper/whiteboard, and ask what they can see? Being winter, it is very possible that someone will suggest it is a snow scene. Announce that you are going to add various pieces to the 'picture' to make things a little clearer. Stick on the various pieces of the snowman, beginning with the body, then the arms, scarf, buttons, head, hat, nose, mouth and eyes, asking each time if anyone can guess what you're making (someone will probably guess early on, if they haven't already done so at the beginning).

Of course, even the heaviest fall of snow doesn't obliterate everything such that all we see is whiteness, as in our original sheet of blank paper, but it does change the way the world looks and feels. (Pull away the sheet of paper, to reveal the winter scene underneath.) No wonder many people feel there's something almost magical about heavy snow, for while it can be both dangerous and a nuisance, it can transform even the most ordinary view into a wonderland, which perhaps explains why both the prophet Isaiah and David in the Psalms used the idea of snow to illustrate the way God's love is able to transform our lives. 'Wash me,' says David in Psalm 51:7, 'and I shall be whiter than snow.' 'Though your sins are like scarlet,' the prophet Isaiah tells us (1:18), 'they shall be like snow.' In other words, however many mistakes we may make, however spoilt our life might be by the things we do wrong, God is able to change us into something beautiful and special, constantly working within us to make us new.

That is a truth at the heart of Advent, with its reminder of the love of God shown in the gift of Christ: the one who 'will save his people from their sins' (Matthew 1:21b). Through him, God accepts us as we are, time and again showing his forgiveness, and through him he helps us to become the people he would have us be. A fall of snow is special, transforming the ordinary into something extraordinary, but the way God in Christ is able to transform lives is more special, more amazing and more wonderful still.

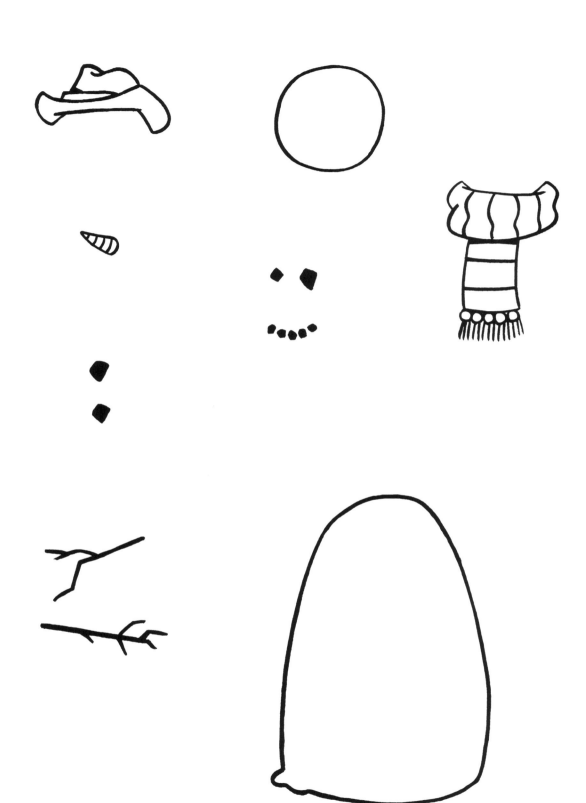

# CHRISTMAS

# A Place in Our Hearts

**Readings**  Luke 2:1-7; John 1:10-13

**Aim**  To ask whether we have made room for Jesus in our daily lives.

**Preparation**  In large bold letters, write or print the following, one per page, at the top of A4-size thick pieces of card:

> JOSEPH, SHEPHERDS, MARY, WISE MEN, HEROD, INN, SCRIBES AND PHARISEES, OWN PEOPLE, YOU AND ME? (2 copies)

Take another piece of card of the same thickness but a different colour, and cut out an irregular shape, large enough to write JESUS in large letters on one side. Make another nine identical copies of this so that you have ten in all. Take the A4 cards labelled JOSEPH, SHEPHERDS, MARY, WISE MEN and YOU AND ME? (first copy), trace around the irregular shape halfway down each piece of card, positioning it differently each time, and then cut around the tracing so that the shape fits nicely into the hole, like the last piece of a jigsaw. Take the A4 cards labelled HEROD, INN, PRIESTS, OWN PEOPLE and YOU AND ME? (second copy) but this time cut just inside one or more of the lines so that there is no way the shape can fit into the resulting space. Rub out any lines that may be left showing from your original tracing. Stick the 10 A4 cards, words facing inwards, on whiteboards or any other suitable vertical surface at the front of the church (making sure you know where the two labelled YOU AND ME? are situated).

Finally, prepare five large red ticks and five large blue crosses (the mathematical rather than religious kind!) out of card or paper.

**Talk**  Explain that you have prepared 10 'jigsaw' pieces, five of which will fit into the holes on the A4 cards and five of which won't. Ask who would like to choose one of the cards and try their luck at fitting in one of the jigsaw pieces. Allow time for volunteers to experiment with different positions for their jigsaw piece, but if the piece clearly does not fit step in, say thank you and stick a blue cross (using sticky tack) over the card. If the piece fits, place a tick over the card.

Continue until every card has either a tick or a cross. Then turn over the jigsaw pieces and cards except the two labelled YOU AND ME?, to reveal the significance of the puzzle. The jigsaw piece in each case represents Jesus, and we see that he found a place in the heart of Mary, Joseph, the shepherds and wise men; but that there was no place for him in the heart of Herod or his own people, nor among the scribes and Pharisees, nor in the inn.

So what of the last two cards: what do they say? Turn these over to reveal the labels YOU AND ME. Here we see simply illustrated the vital challenge of Christmas. Which are we like: those who welcomed Jesus into their lives, joyfully making a place for him, or those in whose lives there was no room? Is there a place in our hearts to receive him?

# What's Missing?

**Readings**     Luke 2:1-16; Matthew 2:1-12

**Aim**     To warn against the danger of losing sight of Jesus as the heart of our Christmas celebrations.

**Preparation**     On a large whiteboard or sheet of paper stuck to a wall, draw the outline of a stable. Then, on A4 sheets of card draw simple outline sketches of the following: angels, three sheep, a star, three wise men, three shepherds, Mary, Joseph, a manger (clearly empty), gold, frankincense and myrrh. Position these conspicuously around the walls of the church. Finally, in large letters, print the following on separate strips of card:

> FRANKINCENSE, SHEEP, STAR, WISE MEN, SHEPHERDS, STABLE, MARY, MANGER, JOSEPH, GOLD, ANGELS, MYRRH

**Talk**     Tell the congregation that you want their help in constructing a Christmas nativity mural from the pictures placed around the church. Explain that you are going to read verses from the Christmas stories of Luke and Matthew, each of which will mention something or someone in one or more of the pictures. The first person to put their hand up with the right answer can bring you the matching picture. (If a verse covers more than one picture, allow others to put their hands up once the first volunteer has brought forward a matching picture.) As each picture is brought forward, fasten it with sticky tack to a large board or piece of paper, gradually building up a simple tableau. Along the edge of the scene, or on a separate board alongside it, place the appropriate word describing the picture (having already positioned the word 'stable'), arranging each as follows:

```
F R A N K I N C E N S E
          S H E E P
      S T A R
          W I S E M E N
            S H E P H E R D S
          S T A B L E
          M A R Y
          M A N G E R
      J O S E P H


    G O L D
          A N G E L S
      M Y R R H
```

The Bible verses are as follows:

- Joseph also went from the town of Nazareth in Galilee to Judea, to the city of David called Bethlehem, because he was descended from the house and family of David. (Luke 2:4) – *Joseph*

- He went to be registered with Mary, to whom he was engaged and who was expecting a child. (Luke 2:5) – *Mary*

- And she gave birth to her firstborn son and wrapped him in bands of cloth, and laid him in a manger, because there was no place for them in the inn. (Luke 2:7) – *manger*

- In that region there were shepherds living in the fields, keeping watch over their sheep by night. (Luke 2:8) – *shepherds* and *sheep*

- And suddenly there was with the angel a multitude of the heavenly host, praising God and saying, 'Glory to God in the highest heaven, and on earth peace among those whom he favours!' (Luke 2:13-14) – *angels*

- In the time of King Herod, after Jesus was born in Bethlehem of Judea, wise men from the East came to Jerusalem, asking, 'Where is the child who has been born king of the Jews?' (Matthew 2:1-2a) – *wise men*

- When they had heard the king, they set out; and there, ahead of them, went the star that they had seen at its rising, until it stopped over the place where the child was. When they saw that the star had stopped, they were overwhelmed with joy. (Matthew 2:9-10) – *star*
- Then, opening their treasure-chests, they offered him gifts of gold, frankincense, and myrrh. (Matthew 2:11b) – *gold, frankincense* and *myrrh*

Run through the list of words and nativity scene, pointing out how the pictures you've assembled go together to make up Christmas Day. But do they? Is anything missing? (Ask the congregation.) The one thing we've forgotten, of course, is Jesus – the baby in the manger. Sometimes at Christmas we can do just that – leave out the one at its centre, the one who it's actually all about. We turn Christmas into an idealised picture of shepherds and wise men kneeling before the manger, or we forget even about these, seeing it simply as an excuse to have a good time. All these have their place, but all are incidental to what Christmas is finally about: the newborn baby, the Word made flesh, the Saviour, the Son of God. Don't let him be missing from your Christmas.

# Have I Got News for You!

**Readings**  Isaiah 52:5-10; Luke 2:8-14

**Aim**  To offer a reminder that the Christmas message applies to us all – it is good news for everyone.

**Preparation**  Collect a selection of newspapers from the past week and cut out a selection of headline articles concerning topical news items. Ensure that these relate to issues spanning a wide variety of countries, continents or places across the world, and, if possible, choose some that younger children may be able to identify and relate to. Display the headlines, deleting a key word or phrase from each and making a list of the deleted words.

**Talk**  Tell the congregation that you are going to play your own version of the TV quiz show *Have I Got News for You?* Show the list of words you have deleted from the selection of headlines you have chosen, and then run through the latter one by one, asking each time if anyone can identify the missing word. We read in our newspapers, or hear and see on television, items of news from across the world. Some of those will directly affect us, others perhaps indirectly, but most will have no real bearing on our daily lives; few issues affect everyone the world over. Our reading today, however, speaks of an event that does just that; an event, of course, that we celebrate once more today: 'I am bringing you good news of great joy for all the people: to you is born this day in the city of David a Saviour, who is the Messiah, the Lord' (Luke 2:10b-11).

Whoever we are and wherever we may be, the message of Christ's birth is, and will always be, good news that can change not only our life but the lives of all those around us – news that still has power to change the world!

# Sharing the News

**Readings**  Luke 2:8-18; John 1:6-9

**Aim**  To emphasise that as well as being news for us (see Talk 9), the message of Christmas is good news for others: news that we have a responsibility to share.

**Preparation**  Print the following in large bold individual letters so that each can be rearranged afterwards, letter by letter, to form an unjumbled word. Using small pieces of sticky tack or magnetic tape, display as below on a whiteboard.

HET LAIDY PHARGLEET

TEH EMITS

THE NUS

YADIL LIAM

TEH REXSESP

EHT ARANGDIU

LINNACIAF SMITE

ETH TINNDEEPEND

ILADY RATS

HET ROBVERSE

SAYNUD MOIRRR

RIGMONN TARS

**Talk**  Tell the congregation that you have jumbled up some newspaper titles. Look at these, one by one; ask if anyone can identify the title.

HET LAIDY PHARGLEET *(The Daily Telegraph)*

TEH EMITS *(The Times)*

THE NUS *(The Sun)*

YADIL LIAM *(Daily Mail)*

TEH REXSESP *(The Express)*

EHT ARANGDIU *(The Guardian)*

LINNACIAF SMITE *(Financial Times)*

ETH TINNDEEPEND *(The Independent)*
ILADY RATS *(Daily Star)*
HET ROBVERSE *(The Observer)*
SAYNUD MOIRRR *(Sunday Mirror)*
RIGMONN TARS *(Morning Star)*

Each of these, with differing degrees of factual accuracy, tells us what's going on in the world around us. They keep us informed of current affairs, both in our own country and further afield. But, of course, not everyone reads newspapers, and in the time when Jesus was born nobody did, for they hadn't been invented then. News in those days was passed by word of mouth, which is precisely what we see in the example of the shepherds. Having been to Bethlehem and seen the child lying in a manger 'they made known what had been told them about this child; and all who heard it were amazed at what the shepherds told them' (Luke 2:17b). The shepherds knew that what had taken place on that night was not simply good news for them but also for all people. Similarly, John the Baptist, whom we heard about in our second reading, proclaimed the good news of Christ, telling all who would listen that here was the Light of the World.

There are some things we can leave to the newspapers, but some things we can't, and one of the latter is the message of the gospel. For one thing, it is no longer seen by the world as news; many imagine they know what it's all about even though they have never heard or responded to that message. Just as important, the picture painted is often twisted and confused, as jumbled as the words we looked at earlier. We need to tell what Jesus means to us, what we have experienced of his love, for there is no substitute for personal testimony, speaking firsthand of what we have seen and know. We have heard again of the 'good news of great joy' for all the people, but as well as hearing it, are we also prepared to share it?

# Worth Pondering

**Reading**    Luke 2:8-19

**Aim**    To encourage people to reflect on the Christmas message rather than simply celebrate the occasion and then forget it.

**Preparation**    Using large letters on a whiteboard or OHP, print the following on one sheet:

> Coming home really is sometimes the ideal solution because on rainy nights few other retreats yield options undercover

> Each was above nil if the squared area sum approximated for two below the ninth digit

> Chewing Tabasco and raw chilli met with impromptu gasps

> The important theme unravels or better appears knowable now in hidden text

**Talk**    Display the first sentence, concealing the rest with a piece of card or paper, and ask if anyone can make sense of it. What is it saying? If nobody spots the hidden message, announce that there is a coded truth concerning Christmas hidden in the sentence. Offer further clues if necessary, though this will almost certainly be unnecessary. The hidden message can be spelt out by taking the first letter of each word in turn, thus making 'Christ is born for you'.

Continue in similar fashion with the next two sentences. By now, the congregation will be alert to what you are doing and should have no trouble spotting the coded messages. In the second sentence this is hidden in the final letter of each word, reading backwards – The word made flesh – and in the third sentence it is hidden in the final letter of each word, but reading forward – 'God with us'. In each sentence there is more than first meets the eye. To anyone prepared to pause and ponder, a whole new meaning appears that wasn't immediately obvious. It's not just in coded sentences that this can be true. We may think we know someone, only to discover hidden depths to their character. We may imagine we have understood something, only to learn new information which forces us to think again. Considered reflection is often needed if we are to see more than just part of the truth.

This, for me, is the truth that emerges from the example of Mary when it comes to Christmas. On the one hand, in our reading, we have the shepherds coming breathless and excited to the stable to see the child the angels told them about, and then rushing out to tell others, leaving them amazed at the good news. On the other hand, we have Mary, who, we read, 'treasured all these words and pondered them in her heart' (Luke 2:19). Did the shepherds and those they spoke to understand the full significance of what had happened? Did they come afterwards to faith in Christ, committing their lives to his service? We do not know, just as we do not know for sure how Mary was later to respond to the life, death and resurrection of her son. What we do know, though, is that in all the trauma, excitement, wonder and mystery of his birth, she made time to stop and think, time to reflect on what it all might mean. And that brings us to the last sentence (display the final sentence and ask if anyone can discover the hidden message – 'think about it' – found through the first letter of each word, but reading backwards.

We do well to learn that lesson in turn, for we can all too easily be so caught up in the fun and festivity of Christmas, even the religious services and celebrations, that we forget to pause quietly and consider what it's all about, what difference it makes to our lives. Enjoy this time and everything that is part of your Christmas, but allow a few moments also each day to consider the events at its heart. Remember that it is about Christ born for you, the Word made flesh, God with us – think about it!

# A Costly Christmas

**Reading**  Luke 2:25-35

**Aim**  This talk, particularly suitable for the week after Christmas, aims to bring home the fact that the coming of Christ into the world involved cost as well as reward. It asks if we are ready to make this season a time of giving as well as receiving.

**Preparation**  On an OHP or whiteboard, display the following riddle in large letters:

> My first is in RICHES, and seen in great PRICE.
>
> My second's in JOHN, and heard in his VOICE.
>
> My third is in TREASURES, at least FRANKINCENSE.
>
> My fourth is in GIFTS, and the wise men's PRESENTS.
>
> My fifth is in CHILD as well as in ONLY.
>
> My last is in MARY, found also in HOLY.
>
> My whole is a word that should help us to know
>
> The love God has given, and the love we should show.

**Talk**  Display the riddle and read it out twice, giving people the opportunity to work out the answer. After allowing a suitable amount of time, ask if anyone has solved it (the answer is COSTLY). Many people may see Christmas as a costly time in the sense of money spent on food, decorations, presents and so forth, but if we look at that first Christmas it involved a different sort of cost. It involved cost to Mary, in allowing herself to be used by God and, as Simeon was to warn her, in subsequent traumas as her son's destiny unfolded. It involved cost to the wise men in the treasures they brought in homage; cost to God in offering his only Son; and cost ultimately to Jesus himself, for he was born to die, to give his life as a ransom for many. Each showed a willingness to give, even to the point of costly sacrifice, and each asks us whether, as well as receiving, *we* are ready to give in turn, ready to accept the cost of discipleship as well as the rewards, ready to take if necessary the path of self-sacrifice and self-denial.

As we share gifts this Christmastime, let us remember how much it cost for Christ to come among us, and let us consider our response to such awesome love.

# EPIPHANY

# Seeing the Light

**Readings**   Matthew 2:1-12; John 1:1-5

**Aim**   To emphasise that through the coming of Jesus light has dawned in the world, scattering the things that can keep us in darkness.

**Preparation**   Print the following words in large bold letters and stick them in prominent positions around the church.

> STAR, TORCH, LIME, FIRE, SEARCH, DAY, CANDLE, HEAD, SPOT, FLASH, FLOOD, MOON, TRAFFIC, SKY, SUN

Finally, on separate strips of card/paper, print the word LIGHT in large bold print 15 times and arrange in a column down the centre of a whiteboard.

**Talk**   Tell the congregation that you have prepared a quiz concerning various types of light, and that to help with the answers there are different words scattered around the church, each of which goes with the word 'light'. Read out the clues below one by one, and ask the first person who puts his or her hand up to bring you the word that matches the answer (given afterwards in italics). Stick this on to a whiteboard and place the word LIGHT alongside it.

1. We look up at these as they twinkle in the night sky – *Starlight*

2. Something we might read by under the blankets as children – *Torchlight*

3. Sounds like a luminous fruit, but refers to being the star of the show – *Limelight*

4. Not bright enough to read by, but it certainly keeps you warm – *Firelight*

5. It sounds like we may have to look hard for the answer to this one – *Searchlight*

6. You won't find this during the night, for it's the complete opposite – *Daylight*

7. We perhaps associate this most with Christmas carol services – *Candlelight*

8. You won't get far driving at night without this – *Headlight*

9. Used in the theatre, or as a metaphor for being the centre of attention – *Spotlight*

10. You'll need this if you're taking photographs indoors – *Flashlight*

11. Not used under water, despite how it might sound – *Floodlight*

12. Just the thing, so they say, for a romantic evening stroll – *Moonlight*

13. You'll be in for a fine or may even lose your licence if you jump this – *Traffic light*

14. Not a light, but a window in the roof that lets light in – *Skylight*

15. Without this light, nothing and none of us would be here – *Sunlight*

These are just some of the things associated with light, and each helps give some idea of how important light is to us and how large a part it plays in our lives. Imagine a house in which there were no lights, or a world in which there was no sun! Many find the short days and long nights of winter hard enough to bear, but if there was no light of any sort at any time, we'd all find life impossible.

Epiphany, though, reminds us of a light more powerful and more important than any of these, more special even than the life-giving rays of the sun itself. It is, of course, the light of Christ; a light able to scatter the darkness of evil and death itself, symbolised at Epiphany by the star that guided wise men from the East. 'What has come into being in him was life,' says John (1:3b-5), 'and the life was the light of all people. The light shines in the darkness, and the darkness did not overcome it.' Or, as Jesus himself puts it in John 8:12, 'I am the light of the world. Whoever follows me will never walk in darkness but will have the light of life.'

Epiphany reminds us that however dark life may seem, however gloomy the world may sometimes appear, God's light will continue to shine until that day when darkness is finally fully overcome in his kingdom and there will be 'no need of sun or moon to shine on it, for the glory of God is its light, and its lamp is the Lamb. The nations will walk by its light, and the kings of the earth will bring their glory into it. Its gates will never be shut by day – and there will be no night there' (Revelation 21:23b-25).

# Transforming the Ordinary

**Reading**   John 2:1-11

**Aim**   To bring home the Epiphany message that Jesus is able to take what seems ordinary and transform it into something special.

**Preparation**   This talk takes a fair bit of work, but it's worth it, the visual effect making a lasting impression. It revolves around the ancient art of origami. You will need several A4-size pieces of thin card – any colour will do, although something bold like red may help the 'models' you're going to make stand out better. You will also need some fast-acting glue or sticky tape, a pencil, a pair of scissors, and a long strip (preferably comprising at least 12 connected pages) of computer paper (used paper, if possible, to avoid unnecessary waste). If you want to save on cutting out during the service, you will also need a thick black marker pen. It is worth practising all of the models at home first to make sure they work on the day; otherwise the results could be embarrassing! To avoid people becoming restless, it is important to talk through what you are doing, showing the congregation what's happening at each stage of the model-making.

**Talk**   Tell the congregation that you've brought along something very ordinary to show them, and hold up your pieces of A4 card. Suggest that what looks ordinary is not, however, always as ordinary as it seems, and then proceed to demonstrate as follows:

Fold one of the pieces of card into quarters and cut one of these out. Fold and then cut this quarter in half length-ways. Take the small rectangle you are left with, and fold this widthways. Your piece of card should now look like this:

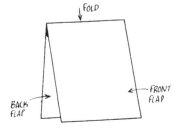

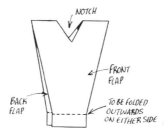

Cut out a notch in the middle of the folded end and trim both edges to make a sort of 'V' shape as illustrated.

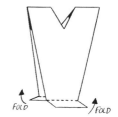

Bend the loose ends outwards on each side, as shown here.

Finally, hold the paper as in the illustration on the left, and, standing close to a microphone, blow hard. The resulting 'whistle' will be well received by youngsters in the congregation and will give any older members who may have dozed off a rude awakening!

A simple whistle, made out of a piece of card. We find the same idea of transforming the ordinary in our reading, though in a much more impressive way. Approached by his mother when supplies of wine run out at a wedding feast, Jesus takes six jars of water and somehow turns them into wine. An astonishing miracle, we might think, but not nearly as astonishing as the truth it symbolises: the fact that Jesus was to transform the life and faith of his nation. And even that is nothing compared to the still greater miracle that Jesus repeatedly performed during his earthly ministry and continues to perform now.

Take a second piece of card and fold it in half and then in half again. Draw a church-window shape in the centre of each segment and door shape at the bottom of one segment and either cut these out or colour them in with a marker pen; then cut crenellations around the top, as follows:

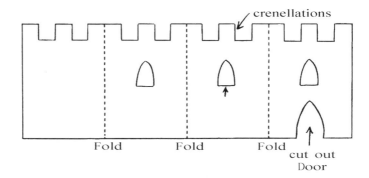

crenellations

Fold     Fold     Fold

cut out
Door

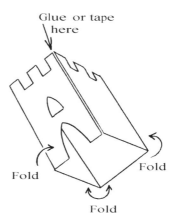

Glue or tape
here

Fold

Fold

Fold

Reverse one of the folds so that the card can then be folded into an oblong shape. Stick down the edges at the top, bottom and centre, as follows:

Stand this up lengthways, to make a tower. Take another piece of card and again fold it in half and then in half again, once more reversing one of the folds so that the card can then be folded into an oblong shape. Before making the oblong, however, cut two inches down each crease and fold the resulting flaps in on themselves. Now fold into an oblong, and stick down the edges and flaps as below:

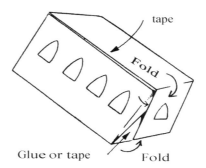

tape

Fold

Glue or tape    Fold

Position the oblong horizontally alongside the tower, as follows:

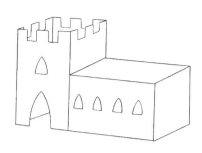

Finally, take another piece of card and fold and cut this in half to form two A5 pieces. Take one of the A5 pieces, and fold it in half lengthways. Cut two inches off one end, then place it over the horizontal oblong, to make a roof. Your model should now look like this.

Ask the congregation what you have created – a church. While we may construct a church building, however, it is God through Jesus who creates the Church, and that is surely one of the greatest miracles of all: the fact that Jesus can make something special out of ordinary people like you and me, transforming them by his love. And that leads to one final bit of paper modelling, for of course the Church isn't about bricks and mortar but about people.

Take the computer paper and, keeping the pages joined together, fold each page in half. With the first fold away from you, cut out a half-figure shape, making sure that your cut goes right across to the other side of the paper, as follows:

TOP FOLD ON THIS SIDE

Ask two volunteers to help you, give them one end of the computer paper each to hold, and gently unravel the 'frieze' you have made, which should look like this:

Again we took what was ordinary and made it into something special, just as God is able to take our lives, take each of us, and use us in a special way, beyond anything we might expect.